Initiate A Plastic Bag Ban

TED DUBOISE

ISBN: **0615972454**
ISBN-13: 978-0615972459

DEDICATION

This book is dedicated to the pioneers of plastic bag bans. These people had the courage to say "no" to plastic bags simply because it made good sense. They saw the future problems with plastic bags before anyone else could see them. With high regards, this book recognizes:

The 1989 members of the Board of Selectmen of Nantucket, Mass who passed the very first plastic bag ban in the U.S.

Peter Captain, Sr. of the Louden Tribal Council who helped pass the Galena, Alaska plastic bag ban in 1998

San Francisco Supervisor Ross Mirkarimi who drafted the ordinance for the first plastic bag ban in a large city in America

CONTENTS

FOREWORD

If only people stopped to consider the side effects of those plastic shopping bags that have been cleverly foisted upon us since the 1970's, we would definitely carry our own reusable shopping bags to the grocery store, just like our grandmothers did before the creation of this ubiquitous man-made product.

Everywhere we look---along our roads, in our trees, in our lakes, rivers and storm drains we see the plastic bag litter. Eventually the rivers and drains carry the bags to the ocean where the bags look like food and are eaten by marine creatures, causing horrific deaths. A Holocaust of the ocean is taking place before our unseeing eyes. Land animals are not immune and they can also eat plastic with equally devastating results.

Until very recently only a few motivated municipalities, cities and counties have implemented a ban or tax on plastic bags.

But now, with step-by-step advice from author, Ted Duboise, in his book, *Initiate A Plastic Bag Ban,* any person or group can organize a movement to rid their community from the plastic bag plague.

Duboise provides the information required to assemble a group of dedicated volunteers motivated to clean up their community, and he guides them through the process of legally establishing a ban on plastic bags. For the persons who no longer want to tolerate a product that is neither good for the ocean, the planet, or all that live on it, this book is a must have.

Follow Duboise's recommendations and implement a plastic bag ban in your community as a first step towards a Zero Waste way of life.

Goffinet McLaren – Author

"Sullie Saves The Seas"

CHAPTER 1
WHAT IS A PLASTIC BAG BAN?

Plastic shopping bags have become ubiquitous with retailers the world over. From the most luxurious shops of Fifth Avenue in New York City to the dustiest of flea markets in small towns across America, merchants and shoppers alike rely on plastic carryout bags for transporting a customer's purchases.

Though extremely thin and lightweight, plastic shopping bags will carry their weight 100 times over, and more. They protect their contents from weather and prevent seepage from leaking products inside as long as there are no holes in the bag.

For over thirty years, merchants have used thin-filmed plastic bags for customers to take home their goods. Plastic bags are cheap; much cheaper than paper bags. Merchants don't charge the customer for the bag as they feel that they are providing a service to their customers. Obviously, customers feel that this is a win-win situation.

However, the merchant must recover the cost in some manner. After all, the merchant is in business to make a profit. As we all know, the cost of the plastic bags is rolled into the price of the merchandise. As the statement goes, "There are no free lunches".

So plastic bags are not free after all.

Another cost that goes with plastic bags is the price of municipal solid waste – the consumer's trash pick-up bill. When a consumer is finished using the plastic bag, he/she tosses the bag into a trash bin or a recycling bin. If the bag is tossed into a trash bin, then the waste is hauled away and deposited into a landfill where the city or county must maintain the storage of waste products.

The cost to maintain storage facilities for trash, i.e. landfills, is enormous. Millions of dollars are spent each year by cities and counties to maintain landfills. Those dollars come from you and I, the taxpayers.

I feel that the only true way to dispose of plastic bags is to recycle them. By recycling plastic, we "return to life" a very useful product in the form of new plastic bags or building products. Percentage-wise, very few plastic bags are recycled. According to the U.S. Environmental Protection Agency (EPA), only about 12% of plastic bags are recycled.(1)

If we try to dispose of plastic bags by "throwing away", we fail miserably. There is no "away" for plastic bags. Plastic does not degrade, it "photo-degrades", meaning it simply breaks into smaller pieces. To degrade, a living organism must eat it. At this time, a living organism that eats plastic hasn't been found.

According to Capt. Charles Moore, the length of time for plastic to degrade can be hundreds of years or longer.(2) I have found no scientific evidence to dispute this. Thus, the euphemism, "Plastic, like diamonds, is forever." Because of this, some say that every piece of plastic ever made is still on the earth.

The Natural Resources Defense Council (NRDC) states: Marine plastic pollution shows us that we cannot really throw anything "away." (3)

Plastic bags are a problem. We can't throw them away and we won't recycle them. If you think plastic bags are not a problem, then why does the federal government (EPA) track their usage and track their recycling rates?

It has been my experience as a businessman that if a problem can't be fixed, then you eliminate the source of the problem.

If we as humans can't dispose of plastic bags properly by putting them in a recycle bin, then we must eliminate plastic bags.

Eliminating plastic bags means to prohibit their use by retailers at checkout. Instituting a plastic bag ban is the solution. So what is a plastic bag ban?

A plastic bag ban is legislation passed by a governing agency to prohibit merchants from providing plastic bags to customers for carrying away purchases. Who passes plastic bag bans? Governing agencies such as municipalities, county governments, state legislatures, and even entire nations ban plastic bags.

As of this writing, there are 168 plastic bag bans in effect in the U.S. All of those bans are by cities and counties because no U.S. state legislature has passed a plastic bag ban. Several states in Australia have passed bans.(4)

So what are the reasons for prohibiting merchants from providing plastic bags to their customers? Why pass a plastic bag ban?

The reasons are numerous. In further chapters, I will discuss in detail the problems with single-use plastic carry-out bags and the many reasons that jurisdictions decide to ban their use.

I want to make it clear that my only reason for banning plastic bags is this: Plastic bags are killing our marine life and sea birds by polluting our oceans and killing land animals which mistake the plastic bags for food. Paper and reusable bags don't do this.

According to UNEP, 80% of ocean pollution is land-based. This means that no matter how far from the ocean you live, an improperly disposed plastic bag will eventually reach the ocean through our rivers and by riding the wind! (8)

∞ Plastic, like diamonds, is forever.
- Unknown

CHAPTER 2
THE PROBLEM WITH PLASTIC BAGS

First of all, the biggest problem is with the sheer volume of bags being used. In 2008, according to the U.S. Dept. of Commerce, the United States consumed 102.1 billion PRCB's (in one year). PRCB is short for "polyethylene retail carrier bag". PRCB is what we call plastic shopping bags.(5)

According to the U.S. Census Bureau, in 2012 there were 115,226,802 households in the U.S. That means that every household used approximately 885 plastic bags per year or 17 plastic bags per week.(6) Since the EPA estimates that only 12% of those plastic bags are recycled (12.2 billion), where does the other 90 billion go?

Do the bags go into our municipal solid waste? Let's go to the EPA. Municipal solid waste (msw) includes all residential, commercial and business trash hauled away each week by the garbage man. In 2011, we as a society generated some 250 million tons of msw, of which 18% was plastic (all plastic, not just bags).

After recovery of materials in the waste stream by recycling and composting, 164 million tons of msw were discarded, of which 18% were plastics. Discarded means the msw was hauled to a landfill. So 29,520,000 tons of plastic was placed in landfills in 2011. Reportedly, about 3% of plastic waste is plastic bags, so 885,600 tons of plastic bags were placed in landfills.

According to the American Chemical Council, a plastic bag weighs 4-5 grams, which is .141096 ounces.(7) This means there is approximately 113 plastic bags in a pound. Therefore, if my math is correct, we placed over 200 million plastic bags into landfills in 2011.

Now obviously, I'm not a scientist or a mathematician, but here I've accounted for only about 12.4 billion of the 102 billion plastic bags used in one year in the United States. Again, I ask, where did the other 90 billion go? I've already established that the bags didn't go "away" because there is no "away".

The "away" usually means our oceans – and lakes and rivers. The plastic bags that are not recycled and don't go into landfills are the ones that litter our landscapes and pollute our rivers and lakes. Eventually, the bags make their way to the ocean via the wind or the rivers and there they remain indefinitely. Could the 90 billion missing plastic bags be in our oceans, rivers and lakes?

The NRDC says that "plastic pollution affects every waterway, sea and ocean" in the world.(3) In 2006, the United Nations Environment Program (UNEP) stated: "Over 46,000 pieces of plastic litter are floating on every square mile of ocean today. In the Central Pacific, there are up to 6 pounds of marine litter to every pound of plankton".(8) That was in 2006, eight years ago; imagine what the statistics are now.

Plastic bags cause other problems with the environment and cause problems with nature. After the plastic gets into the ocean, it begins to break down more and more until it is small bits and fragments. These tiny fragments are ingested by fish because they look like food.

Plastic bags floating in the pelagic environment appear as jellyfish to loggerhead turtles. Turtles love jellyfish; therefore they ingest the plastic bags. Sea birds dive into the water to pick up the tiny fragments of plastic thinking they are food. They eat the plastic or fly back to their nest to feed their young. Thousands die each year because they mistake the floating plastic for food.

The plastic that is ingested by fish, turtles, or seabirds blocks the digestive system, thereby causing death by starvation.

Death by plastic affects not only our marine life but also our land-based animals, which, like marine animals, mistake bags for food.

Across the globe, in the United Arab Emirates, plastic waste is killing wildlife and domestic animals in alarming numbers. "This is the worst environmental threat facing this country," stated Dr. Ulrich Wernery, Scientific Director of the Central Research Veterinary Laboratory. "Death of our animals from plastic is reaching epidemic proportions in the UAE."(9)

Plastic bags also wreak havoc for America's cotton farmers. The U.S. Cotton Industry must ensure that it supplies "pure" cotton. Only non-contaminated cotton is used to make the finest cotton fabric. An excerpt from a report by The Journal of Cotton Science in 2008 which explores the problem of cotton that is contaminated by plastic bags blowing into the fields and not removed before the cotton is harvested sheds light on the situation:

"**D**amage claims exceeding \$5,000,000 annually have been filed against US spinning mills when contaminants have spoiled the retail value of finished goods (National Cotton Council, 1997).

The majority of contamination objects that end up in yarn come from plastic in the field. For example: Dale Fite, vice president of fiber operations, Harriet & Henderson Yarns stated "The most frequent contaminant we've found in eastern cotton is Wal-Mart bags; those blue plastic bags.... Careless littering is putting a tremendous amount of contamination in cotton fields. This is creating a problem for farmers, for yarn spinners and for our customers (Hudson, 2000)."(10)

The problems that plastic bags create exist all over the world. There are many more than the ones I've listed above but these give you an idea of the situation.

Numerous citizens across the U.S. are also concerned about the problems with plastic bags. Many people have contacted me asking "How can I start a plastic bag ban in my town or community?"

So many people have asked for this information and this is why I have produced this book. Here is the information that anyone can use to initiate a plastic bag ban.

CHAPTER 3
ORGANIZE A TEAM

Starting and managing a campaign to ban plastic bags is no easy task! It is not for the faint-hearted or lazy person. It is, and will be hard work. You must decide the level of your commitment. Will you see it through to a ban – or will you just initiate the actions and turn everything over to someone else to complete?

If you are here at this point, obviously you already feel the need for banning plastic bags, paper bags, or both. I don't have to lay out the reasons. However, I will try to help you look at other reasons for a ban. Maybe I can interject some ideas that might fit your situation or surrounding environment that will give you more reasons for a ban. The more reasons – the better.

In this guide, I will lay out a plan, an outline. However, this is only a basic plan. You, your volunteers, and your supporters must put the plan into action and always look for ways to enhance the plan. Every situation is different – stay alert and be aware of opportunities. Change the plan as needed but let nothing deter you. Once you set the plan into motion, see it through.

This plan is drawn from four years of studying plastic bag bans across the U.S. and talking with the hard-working people behind those bans. Great plans are just that.

It's the people that make the difference! Ironically, it's people that have made the situation with plastic bags and its people who will change it!

The first step to getting started is to organize a team of like-minded people who will work with you to achieve your goal. You may only have two or three people to help you get started but more people will join you as you get the momentum going.

In Bellingham, Washington, two ladies decided that they wanted a plastic bag ban in their town. Brookes Anderson and Jill McIntyre Witt started the ball rolling. Then they engaged the help of Seth Fleetwood, a City Councilman. "We have plans for a Citizen Awareness & Education Outreach throughout the community," stated Ms. Anderson when I interviewed her. A Facebook page was set up and the ladies started talking to others in the community. Then they went to the local newspaper which did a front page article about their idea. They worked hard, never gave up, and four months after starting, a plastic bag ban was passed by the city. In fact, Bellingham's ordinance was used as a model for Seattle's ordinance.(4)

On the Gulf Coast, Rose Timmer and her non-profit, Healthy Communities of Brownsville, spearheaded a grassroots effort to get a plastic bag ban passed in Brownsville, Texas. Brownsville is a border town with Mexico.

Timmer and her volunteers worked two years on the process. After a year, in September, 2009, they formed an environmental advisory committee and started meeting weekly. The group held litter clean-ups then counted the number of plastic bags collected to prove the bags were the city's main source of litter. They conducted surveys and worked with city attorneys to draft an ordinance.(4)

On January 6, 2010, the City Commission of Brownsville passed an ordinance banning single use plastic bags by retailers. Brownsville's ordinance also became a model for other cities in Texas such as South Padre Island and Laguna Vista.

Madeleine Sandefur decided that her town should ban plastic bags. She was lucky enough to meet two members of the local Sierra Club who agreed with her.

After two years of the three working together on several projects for the city along with pressing for the plastic bag ban, the town of Laguna Vista, Texas passed a plastic bag ban ordinance.(4)

Organizing a team could simply mean getting two or three others to work with you or you can build an organization of ten people or more. Obviously, the more people that you have the easier it is to multiply your efforts.

To build your team, talk with members of the community, members of your church or a civic organization. Go to local environmental events and discuss your ideas with attendees.

Talk with youth groups at schools and in the community. In recent years, youth groups have been responsible for plastic bag bans and disposable bag regulations. In Boulder, Colorado, students at Fairview High School and Summit Middle School pressed the city council for a plastic bag ban. Eventually, the Boulder City Council adopted a ten cents fee on plastic and paper disposable bags instead of an outright ban on plastic bags.

∞ 90 Billion plastic bags are missing. Are they in the ocean?

CHAPTER 4
LAYING THE GROUNDWORK

Now that you have your team put together, it's time to build a foundation that will support your plan. As with any type goal, you need a plan to get there. However, before laying out your plan, you need facts and knowledge to fortify your actions.

To be successful with a bag ban, you need a reason or a purpose for banning bags. When you talk to people about banning plastic shopping bags, the first question you'll be asked is "Why?"

Some of the questions will be: "Why should we ban bags?" and "What's the reason for banning bags?" You need to have the answer ready. Clearly know, and be able to state, the reasons or purpose for a plastic bag ban. Will you ban only plastic bags or both plastic and paper (all disposable, single-use bags)?

Be able to tell the person immediately why your town, city or county should ban plastic bags or both paper and plastic bags.

Once you've completed your research as outlined in this chapter, you'll have several reasons for banning disposable bags. Furthermore, you will not only have the reasons but you will have the research to fortify your purpose.

To help decide on the "purpose", I have noted here several reasons that are usually listed at the beginning of many plastic bag ban ordinances. You may use these to get started, but prove each one through your research.

Plastic bags should be banned because:

1. they contribute to overburdened publicly financed landfills, degrade the river and other natural landscapes;
2. they clog storm water drains and sewer lines, necessitating expensive repairs to the Town's infrastructure;
3. they are a significant and costly component of litter;
4. they clog recycling machinery, causing delays and adding repair costs;
5. they are consumed in extremely high volumes;
6. they are produced from non-renewable resources;
7. they are designed to be disposable (rather than reusable);
8. they are difficult to recycle;
9. they are not degradable in the environment;
10. they represent a significant hazard to marine animals, sea birds, and farm animals;
11. they are a nuisance and an eyesore detracting from the beauty of (your city).

Doing research is not complicated. For example, purpose number one listed above can be researched by going to your city's or county's Dept. of Solid Waste. There, you can get facts about plastic bags going into the landfill. How much of a problem is this locally? How much of a problem do plastic bags cause at the local recycling facility? Do they clog the recycling machinery? (Trust me – they do.)

If there is a local river, go check it out. How many plastic bags are visible along the river banks or in the water? Do a local 'river clean up' project and get local citizens involved.

As part of your data, here is some information that most plastic bag ban proponents don't want you to know about. I include it here as part of your research because you need to know. Someone will inevitably ask about this and you need to be able to respond. How you respond is your choice, but I want you to know.

In 2007, the Progressive Bag Alliance, which is backed by the American Chemical Council, commissioned a life-cycle analysis of three types of grocery bags. According to the report, plastic bags are the greener option at checkout.(11) Keep in mind, this study was done for the American Chemical Council.

You can read the report and make your own decision. However, I will tell you that no matter how many studies are done to prove that a plastic bag is greener, there is no study that will prove that plastic bags do not kill marine life, sea birds, and land animals. In fact, plenty of studies prove that they do.

Also in your research, include the following:

1. Area Stats: Know stats about your town, city, county or state.
   a. Population;
   b. Number of plastic bags used yearly (survey retailers);
   c. What local entity or which dept. of city would be in charge of plastic bag regulation (i.e., Dept. of Natural Resources, Dept. of Environmental Quality, Dept. of Public Works, Solid Waste, etc);
   d. How many storm drains are clogged by plastic bags and what is the damage caused by clogged storm drains;
   e. Are there local plastic bag or paper bag manufacturing facilities? If so, number of employees and what effect a ban would have on plant staffing.

2. State laws: Check your state's environmental laws. In some states, such as California and New York, plastic bag bans may be subject to an environmental assessment to state how the action will affect the environment. In California, after several lawsuits against early adopters of bans, the courts decided that plastic bag bans generally aren't subject to the State's CEQA laws. In New York, in the past, bans have not been subject to the SEQR laws. Again, check your state to ensure that you know what to expect.

3. Outreach:
   a. To local businesses (survey: in person or group meetings);
   b. To local citizens (survey: in person, by meetings);
   c. To Retail Associations;
   d. To local recyclers (do they accept and/or recycle plastic bags).

Talk to each group of people and get their input. Do not leave out anyone, especially retailers. You will need their support.

Laying the groundwork is simply defining the problem and then finding the solution. The problem is plastic bags or disposable bags of any type. The solution to the problem is to ban the free distribution of plastic bags.

Of course, there are those individuals who firmly believe that it is their "right" to be able to get a plastic bag from a merchant if they so choose. They feel plastic bags should not be banned.

In our society, when a problem arises that isn't solved by the perpetrators, generally laws are passed to ensure that the solution to the problem is applied by society-at-large.

Seat-belts are a great example. Years ago, studies and tests were conducted to determine the effectiveness of seat-belt usage. It was determined that using seat-belts did, in fact, save lives.

A great campaign was conducted across the nation and in most states to convince people to use seat-belts. After all, it was in the individual's best interest to wear a seat-belt because it could possibly save his/her life if involved in a car accident. Did people readily and willingly embrace the idea and start wearing a seat-belt?

Absolutely not. Not everyone. Even though the facts pointed out that a person's chances of survival if they were involved in an automobile accident were X% greater when wearing a seat-belt, people still didn't buckle up. Even the threat of death didn't force some people to be compliant.

So then, laws were passed to force people to improve their chances of living through an auto accident. Some people still feel that it is their choice whether or not to buckle up for their own safety. But society as a whole passed laws to protect the general population.

Plastic bag bans are looked at in the same manner. If we won't buckle up for our own safety, we certainly won't refuse a plastic bag in order to save a wild animal, our oceans, or the environment. Society as a whole is beginning to realize the damage that plastic bags are doing and are passing laws to prohibit the use of plastic bags by retailers at checkout.

In this next chapter, I will outline an action plan to get you and your team started towards banning plastic bags in your area.

∞ The majority of contamination objects that end up in yarn come from plastic in the field. This is creating a problem for farmers, for yarn spinners and for our customers.

CHAPTER 5
SET YOUR PLAN OF ACTION

Get yourself and your team organized. Go back through the previous chapter and list each of the items in the order of importance. Determine which one of your team will accomplish each item and establish a timeline to have all the information and research completed.

The next step is to formally organize all of the material so that it is easily and quickly accessible. A laptop computer or a tablet is a good place to store your information. These are portable devices that you can take with you to meetings or presentations so that you can have the information readily available. When you need to reference the material to answer questions, you will be prepared.

After organizing the facts and statistics from your research, start your campaign. Set your plan of action to progressively move from the beginning to the final result (ban).

Here is a progressive plan of action that will help you get started. However, you must build upon this plan. Use the plan as a base, then adjust the plan to your needs. There are usually unforeseen circumstances that will come up which you must deal with before moving on. Accept these moments simply as a challenge and opportunity. Don't let them stop you from continuing.

Assign each team member an area of the plan as her/his responsibility. He/she will be responsible for achieving the goals set for that item, including the tasks and timeline. At your group meetings, each person will report their progress and new proposals.

Basic Plan of Action

1. Organize and Commit. Get your team assembled.
2. Research. Get the facts and statistics.
3. Organize facts and statistics from your research material.
4. Organize your Campaign. Determine what you consider your best route to success. If you know someone at City Hall, you might start by discussing your goals with that person. Be prepared for rejection, but do not accept it. Move forward with your plans if that person is cold to the idea.
5. Communication. I recommend setting up a website. Set up a Facebook page but use your website to list all the facts and statistics. You can keep the community informed by posting regular updates to your website.
6. Petition. Create a petition that people can sign to show their commitment. Keep those signed petitions on file. You will need them later. Post your petition on your website so that more people can see it. They can also copy the petition, sign it, and send it to their City Council member.
7. Look for key opportunities to present your campaign to the community. Always have your campaign materials available. Always have petitions on hand. Key opportunities include:
   - Fairs & Festivals: Set up a booth or tables. Great exposure for your campaign;
   - Civic Events: Get on the roster as a speaker on environmental issues;
   - Charity Events: Explain your cause;
   - Business Expos: Great place to present to the business community and local retailers;
   - Chamber of Commerce and their Events: Another great place to present to businesses;
   - Local Businesses: Ask local merchants who favor your campaign to allow you to set a table on their sidewalk on Friday or Saturday. Staff the table with your most enthusiastic team members;
   - River Clean-Ups or Street Clean-Ups: Always participate in these events to show your commitment to the environment and the local area. When possible, count and track the number of plastic bags collected to help show why the plastic bag ban is needed.

- Photos: Make photos of your activities at events and post them on your website to keep the community updated on your campaign;
- Press Releases: You or someone on your team should learn to write press releases about your campaign. Submit the press releases to local media including newspapers, television and radio stations;
- Host a "Bag It" film screening: Many cities have done this with great success. Audiences quickly relate to the way this film explains the problem with plastic bags. See the "Resources" section at the end of this book.

8. Organize Community Meetings: Utilize the first meeting as mostly informational. Present your campaign and explain why you are promoting a plastic bag ban. Answer all questions by attendees. Future meetings will be updates on progress.

9. Organize Business Meetings: Invite all retailers to attend. Discuss the pros and cons of bag regulations. Visit as many retailers as possible to let them know about the meeting and ask them to attend. Business owners will be more apt to get on board if you explain the economics to them. The economics for a business are simply this. Plastic bags cost the merchant about two cents. Paper bags cost about twelve cents. So when you ban plastic bags, people will automatically switch to paper bags, costing the store owner tremendously more money. To offset this higher operating cost, you must impose a fee for the paper bags. The fee can range from a nickel to a quarter, but whatever the amount, it keeps the merchant from losing money because of a plastic bag ban.

∞ "We have plans for a Citizen Awareness & Education Outreach throughout the community", stated Ms. Anderson.

CHAPTER 6
ELEMENTS OF AN ORDINANCE

Let me start by stating that I am not an attorney. I do not dispense legal advice. Any ordinance will have to be written and approved by the city's own legal counsel or county attorney.

The first decision you must make is the type of bag regulations that you wish to include in the ordinance. I have watched various ordinances implemented and then checked the results of those ordinances. The most effective type of regulations has been to ban plastic bags and regular paper bags.

Ordinances in which plastic bags are banned and a fee or charge is placed on recyclable paper bags have achieved the best results in reducing the use of disposable bags. Typically, jurisdictions impose a five cents or ten cents fee but some are as high as twenty-five cents. See the "Resources" section at the end of this book to see different types of plastic bag regulations.

In Chapter 4, I listed several reasons for banning plastic bags. At the beginning of most ordinances, there is a list of justifications for the ordinance, or "purpose and intent". I call this the preamble.

The preamble is the introductory part of the statute that states the reason for and the intent of the law. It is basically a set of statements that explains the problem that is to be regulated. It also usually indicates what is to follow.

Some preambles are very short and others are very long.

Westport, Connecticut's ordinance begins with simply two lines of text explaining the "Purpose". The "Justification" is another two lines. The preamble is direct and to the point.

Here are other examples for the preamble:

WHEREAS, the City of (XX) has a duty to protect the natural environment, the economy and the health of its citizens,

WHEREAS, the use of plastic shopping bags has a significant impact on the environment such as contributing to unsightly litter on the streets, sidewalks, beaches, clogging sewers and drainage systems, and polluting waterways,

WHEREAS, plastic shopping bags are difficult to recycle and currently contaminate material that is processed through the composting program,

WHEREAS, costs associated with the use and disposal of plastic shopping bags creates a burden on the city's solid waste disposal process;

WHEREAS, plastic shopping bags have significant environmental impacts each year, and use of over 12 million barrels of oil for bags in the U.S.,

WHEREAS, plastic shopping bags cause the death of an enormous number of marine animals,

WHEREAS, it is in the best interest of the health, safety, and welfare of the residents of (city) to reduce the cost to the city of solid waste disposal, and to protect the environment by banning the use of plastic checkout bags;

WHEREAS, plastic carryout bags constitute a high percentage of litter, which is unsightly, costly to clean up, and causes serious negative environmental impacts;

WHEREAS, the City has a substantial interest in protecting its residents and the environment from negative impacts from plastic carryout bags;

After the preamble is usually the 'definitions' section. Here, you will define all pertinent terms within the ordinance.

Words that need to be defined include:
- Plastic bag
- Single-use carryout bag
- Disposable bag
- Store
- Retailer
- Retail business
- Reusable bag
- Recyclable paper bag
- Operator
- Customer
- Post-consumer recyclable material
- Recyclable
- Product bag
- Produce bag
- Point of sale

Keep in mind that you may not need all the terms above. Some of the terms are redundant so use the one that fits best.

Next, state what the ordinance does:
- No store shall provide to any customer a plastic carryout bag. *(or)*
- No Retail Establishment shall provide a Single-Use Carry-Out Bag to a Customer, at the check stand, cash register, point of sale or other point of departure for the purpose of transporting food or merchandise out of the establishment except as provided in this Section. *(or)*
- Thin-film single-use plastic bags shall not be distributed, used, or sold for check-out purposes at any retail establishment within the city limits of (city, county). *(or)*
- No retail establishment shall provide or make available to a customer a single-use plastic carryout bag *(or)*
- All stores, shops, food vendors, and restaurants shall provide only the following as checkout bags to customers: recyclable paper bags or reusable bags.

The next section of the ordinance will state and define "permitted bags" and/or list "exemptions".

Examples include:

- All stores shall provide or make available to a customer only recyclable paper carryout bags or reusable bags for the purpose of carrying away goods or other materials from the point of sale, subject to the terms of this Chapter. Nothing in this Chapter prohibits customers from using bags of any type that they bring to the store themselves or from carrying away goods that are not placed in a bag, in lieu of using bags provided by the store.

- Exemptions include: product bags used inside a store for fruits, vegetables, meats; newspaper bags; laundry/dry cleaning bags; door hanger bags; bags sold in packages containing multiple bags intended for use as garbage, pet waste, or yard waste bags.

- No retail establishment shall provide customers with plastic checkout bags less than 2.25 mils thick with the exception of restaurants involved in take-out business. Stores that are using compostable plastic bags may continue to do so.

- All stores must provide, at the point of sale, free of charge, either reusable bags or recyclable paper carryout bags, or both, to any customer participating in the Supplemental Food Program, the federal Supplemental Nutrition Assistance Program, or the WIC program.

The next section of the ordinance will state any pass-through cost or fee that will be charged. Examples:

- Any store that provides a recyclable paper carryout bag to a customer must charge the customer ten cents ($.10) for each bag provided, except as noted in this Chapter.

- No store shall rebate or otherwise reimburse a customer any portion of the ten cents charge required in Subsection A, except as otherwise noted in this Chapter.

- All stores must indicate on the customer receipt the number of recyclable paper carryout bags provided and the total amount charged for the bags.

Enforcement is the next part of the ordinance. Who will enforce this statute? Which city or county agency will be charged with monitoring compliance to the ordinance? This section will also state the actions that will be taken against any violator of the law.

In some jurisdictions, the City/County Compliance Officer or Code Enforcement Officer will be responsible for monitoring compliance to the law. In other jurisdictions, this responsibility will be that of an employee of the Public Works Dept., Solid Waste Dept., or even the Health Dept.

Typically, on the first occurrence of a violation, a compliance warning will be issued. If a violation occurs again, a penalty will be levied. A larger penalty will be levied against the violator if another offense occurs. Eventually, a business that refuses to comply with the law will have their business license suspended or revoked.

The last section of the ordinance will be the Effective Date. Many ordinances basically leave this blank by stating, "This ordinance shall become effective and in full force six months/one year/three months from the passage date. This allows City Council members or the County Board enough time to do their due diligence. Other ordinances state a specific date that the act will go into effect. By leaving the Effective Date at a future time, the City has time to execute a Citizens Awareness or Education program.

The above are the basic elements of an ordinance. Many ordinances include more than just the basics. The length of an ordinance may be very long or very short. The length will be determined by the various laws in a specific jurisdiction. I have included specific ordinances that are now in effect in various parts of the U.S. in the "Resources" section. Studying these will give you a better understanding of ordinances.

I must state again that I am not an attorney and I do not give legal advice. Any ordinance must be drafted by a qualified legal attorney. City or county ordinances are usually drafted by a team or staff of legal attorneys employed by that jurisdiction.

CHAPTER 7
GET CITY HALL'S ATTENTION

I often get the question, "How do I get City Hall's attention?" Many times, this is not easily accomplished. The simple answer is to persuade a Council member to believe in your cause and join the campaign.

When this isn't possible, there are many steps to take before going to City Hall or to the County Board of Supervisors. The key is to have your facts, data, and citizen involvement documented so that when you do contact your local governing agency, you will have a fortified case to present. In fact, if you and your team work your campaign properly, someone from these agencies will contact you because they want to have a role in most anything that their constituents want.

Visit the website of your local City Council member or County Supervisor and take note of the issues she/he is pushing. Check that person's voting record to see if he/she advocates for environmental issues. Does she/he vote for issues affecting the local rivers/creeks, water supply or solid waste. Does he/she push for laws that reduce the environmental impact of pollution from local factories or businesses? Is she/he a strong supporter of local schools?

These things give you a better understanding of your local government representatives. Knowing what each one is most interested in will help you in knowing how to approach her/him.

Here are documents and actions that will cause your local government to take notice of your campaign. Any or all of these will facilitate you getting your campaign to city hall.

1. Documentation of any and all meetings with groups of local citizens. Note the responses and comments that you have received concerning the idea of banning plastic bags. Endorsements by local leaders are always good.

2. Documentation of responses from local businesses. As you canvass your local business owners, get statements from them when you receive positive responses to your campaign. Track and calculate the percentage of negatives to positives. Business owners are similar to politicians in the fact that they desire to give their customers what they want. This helps to keep them in business. If enough of their customers bring reusable bags to shop, most likely they can persuade the business to get on board with you in banning plastic bags and promoting reusable bags.

3. Petitions will be a tremendous asset. The more signed petitions that you have, the more persuasion power you will have at city hall. A petition is a powerful tool. In fact, in some jurisdictions, if you have enough petitions signed by local qualified voters, you can force the issue to be put on a ballot and voted on by citizens. There are many examples where signed petitions effected a change in local laws. Have plenty copies of your petition readily available and don't be shy about asking anyone for a signature. Keep all the signed petitions on file and take them with you when you go to your City Council or County Supervisors. Post a copy of your petition on your website so that people that you may not come in contact with will be able to sign the petition and send it to you. It is nice to get out-of-town visitors to sign the petition but keep in mind that the only petitions usually accepted at City Hall are the ones signed by local citizens and registered qualified voters. There is an example petition in the "Resources" section.

4. Local media is very good for getting noticed also. Send press releases about upcoming meetings or events to your local newspaper and television stations. Ask a reporter to cover your events and write a story for their publisher.

5. Attend City Council meetings and/or meetings of the County Supervisors. Register to be a speaker when a public hearing is held on issues that relate to your campaign. When your issue comes before the Council, you will be recognized as having spoken before. Speaking at previous meetings also gives you an edge on being comfortable to speak on your issues. Most speakers are only allowed three minutes so script what you want to say so that the Council hears the most important items before your time expires.

Ultimately, you must get on the City Council's Agenda Docket. How to do this will vary by jurisdiction. Do your research to learn how this works. Find out who you must talk to and what material is needed. In most cities, you must go through the City Clerk or the City Administrator's office. Simply do whatever is needed. You will probably be rejected the first time, second time, or third time that you try. Each time you are rejected, ask what else you need to do or what other documentation is needed. Then do what you're told to do or get the documentation that you're told is needed.

In one jurisdiction in which I managed a business, I attended several County Commission meetings just to watch the process and learn their procedures. When I needed a variance to the Commission's sign ordinance, I already knew what to expect. I had all documents ready for presentation and was prepared for the questions that were asked. I received the variance.

∞ Plastic bags are a significant hazard to marine animals, sea birds, and farm animals.

CHAPTER 8
SUMMARY

In this book, I have stated the facts about plastic bags. I have laid out a plan that you can use to initiate a plastic bag ban in your home town or county. What you do with this book now is literally in your hands. But I will tell you – the oceans are still full of plastic pollution.

If you decide that running a campaign to ban plastic bags is too big for you to undertake, please pass this book along to someone else. Become a team member with that person and help work the campaign under her/his leadership.

If you don't do it, I believe someone else will. By the year 2020, you will not get a thin-film plastic bag to carry your purchases home. Plastic bag bans or disposable bag bans will be so common place that those jurisdictions that still use plastic bags will only number a few.

I don't believe that we will return to the paper bag. Trees that are currently used in paper bag production will be needed to build homes and businesses. The plastic bag ban movement has caused consumers, manufacturers, and packaging companies to take a new look at how our purchases are transported.

It is possible that the new, thicker mil reusable plastic bags will be commonplace. However, extended producer responsibility laws will be passed that will require the plastic industry to reclaim 80% of their product at end of life. Those type laws are already in existence in Europe and similar laws are in place here in the U.S. for automobile tires and batteries.

I have long contended that the plastic industry has the solution.

With all the wizardry that it takes to mix the chemicals that plastic is made from, and with the wisdom and know-how to make a product that is practically indestructible and last for hundreds of years – yes – they know how to make their product go away. One day they will be forced to do that and then the plastic pollution in our oceans will be reduced.

∞ 90 Billion plastic bags are missing. Are they in the ocean?

CHAPTER 9

RESOURCES

Articles and news of plastic bag bans and plastic pollution:
- PlasticBagBanReport.com
- The PlasticFreeTimes.com
- Rise Above Plastics – surfrider.org
- EcoWatch.com
- CAWrecycles.org

Jurisdictions with plastic bag bans – info and background:
- http://www.sanjoseca.gov/index.aspx?NID=1526

- https://austintexas.gov/department/single-use-carryout-bag-ordinance-documents

- http://www.co.thurston.wa.us/solidwaste/bags/bags-home.html

- http://www.eugene-or.gov/plasticbags

Bag Regulation Results:

- Plastic Bag Ban Report

- L.A. County: http://dpw.lacounty.gov/epd/aboutthebag/

- Santa Monica: smgov.net. Search for "Sustainable City Report Card 2012"

- D.C.: ddoe.dc.gov. Search for "2013 Bag Law Survey Final Report"

Books

- Plastic Ocean – Capt. Charles Moore

- Plastic: A Toxic Love Story – Susan Freinkel

- Plastic Free: How I kicked The Plastic Habit – Beth Terry

- Sullie Saves The Seas – Goffinet McLaren

Movie Screenings:

- "Bag It" The Movie – bagitmovie.com

- "Plastic Paradise" – plasticparadisemovie.com

Educational Outreach Programs for Schools:

- www.ConservingNow.com

Consultants, Economic Impact Studies, EIR:

- http://www.tischlerbise.com/

- AECOM.com

Government Information:

- EPA.gov

- Commerce.gov

Retail Associations:

- California Grocers Association

- Washington State Retailers Association

- National Retail Federation

Websites:

I can help you built a website for your campaign at a very reasonable cost. The site can be pre-loaded with plastic bag facts and data. I will help you research your area so that you have relevant information about the problem in your specific city or county. I will teach you how to update the site on a regular basis to keep the citizens of your city informed.

My contact information is listed at the end of this book.

Petition: I mentioned earlier in the book about the importance of using petitions as part of your campaign. On the next page is a sample petition that you may use or build upon. To copy and paste the petition, go to banplasticbag.com or visit http://gotmybag.com.

CHAPTER 10
PETITIONS

Dear (insert name of City Councilor or Board Commissioner),

Help keep our rivers, lakes and streets clean and reduce plastic's impact on the environment. I am asking you to reduce the amount of plastic waste that goes into our City landfill.

I believe that the City/County of (XX) should prohibit the use of disposable shopping bags and promote the use of reusable shopping bags. Four plastic bags can be eliminated for every one reusable bag that is used.

Some of America's largest cities have already committed to reducing their impact on the environment by passing laws to prohibit the use of plastic and disposable shopping bags. Those cities include Los Angeles, the 2nd largest city in America; San Jose, California, the 10th largest city; and Austin, Texas, the 11th largest city in the U.S. Thus far, 168 jurisdictions across the U.S. have passed plastic and paper bag regulations.

As a citizen of (XX) and your constituent, I urge you to consider legislation to prohibit the use of disposable shopping bags by all businesses in the city. To be fair, all retailers must be included in the law, not just grocery stores, convenience stores, and pharmacies.

Thank you for your time today. I look forward to working with you on this important issue affecting our city.

Signed:

ABOUT THE AUTHOR

Ted Duboise has published Plastic Bag Ban Report for over four years. Plastic Bag Ban Report (PBBR) is a repository of plastic bag bans across the U.S. and throughout the world. The publication is a library of information about plastic bag bans that can easily be referenced to find laws, facts and data.

Visit PlasticBagBanReport.com. Contact info is there also.

PBBR is strictly fact-based. Publishing only the facts means that if information cannot be verified, the story isn't published.

Ted Duboise has been a businessman for the past forty years. For the last twenty years he has resided in the Atlanta, Georgia area.

REFERENCES:

1. U.S.EPA:
   http://www.epa.gov/wastes/conserve/materials/pla
   stics.htm
2. Algalita.org, FAQ's,
   http://www.algalita.org/AlgalitaFAQs.htm
3. NRDC: http://www.nrdc.org/oceans/plastic-
   ocean/
4. Plastic Bag Ban Report,
   http://plasticbagbanreport.com
5. U.S.Dept.ofCommerce:
   http://www.usitc.gov/publications/701_731/pub40
   80.pdf
6. U.S. Census Bureau:
   http://quickfacts.census.gov/qfd/states/00000.html
7. American Chemical Council:
   http://plasticbagfacts.org/Main-Menu/Fast-
   Facts/index.html
8. UNEP.org:
   http://www.unep.org/Documents.Multilingual/Def
   ault.asp?DocumentID=480&ArticleID=5300&l=en
9. Gulf News, 2007.
   http://gulfnews.com/news/gulf/uae/general/death
   -valley-plastic-tragedy-1.463655
10. USDA:
    http://naldc.nal.usda.gov/download/21353/PDF
11. Boustead Consulting & Associates: "Life Cycle
    Assessment for Three Types of Grocery Bags—
    Recyclable Plastic; Compostable, Biodegradable
    Plastic; and Recycled, Recyclable Paper," 2007.

www.ingramcontent.com/pod-product-compliance
Lightning Source LLC
Chambersburg PA
CBHW060702280326
41933CB00012B/2269